ANNY IKEBUDU

LOVE NOT ENOUGH

LESSONS FOR THE LADIES

"DO NOT MARRY YET" SERIES

Love Not Enough
Copyright: © 2016 Anny Ikebudu
Mobile: +2348033207242

First Published by Reveal Publishing, 2016

Revised Edition Published by Global Reach Publishing LLC, 2016

ISBN: 9785033740
ISBN-13: 978-9785033748

Printed in the United States of America

Illustrations:
1. Uduak Akpan
2. Splendid Media Studios
Cover image credit: Dreamstime. Duly Paid for

This work is dedicated to every *single-and -searching* person who is desirous of a good and happy marriage. My desire and *prayer* for you is that it will happen for you soonest in Jesus' name.

CONTENTS

Many thanks to Vivian Beulah Igbokwe who worked on the initial manuscript.

Also, special appreciation to Akinwunmi Adebayo, *conceptual* copywriter at Reveal Publishing, Lagos, Nigeria, who managed this project from the raw manuscript stage to what you now have in your hands. He was simply brilliant.

A Marriage decision is one of the most important decisions a person will make in life. When it is hastily done, the chances of making a regretful choice can be very high. The consequences affects almost every other area of one's life. It is therefore imperative that care and caution is exercised before you get into it. No need to hurry. Don't marry him just yet. A few things to still consider.

CHAPTER ONE

When a Woman Loves a Man

A BEAUTIFUL STORY BEGINS

Aba is a small notable commercial town located in Abia State in South-East Nigeria.

The sun woke up earlier than usual this saturday morning as the familiar Aba weather quickly reminded everyone that it was that time of the year when the ubiquitous dust hung on everything in sight. The gradual warmth bellowing out of the eastern rising sun, a reminder that the clock was ticking and that the day indeed had begun, only hastened the activities of the morning. *Aha!* Finally, the day they had all eagerly waited for had arrived and Adaobi the beautiful bride will be the centre of attraction. After an elaborate *Igba Nkwu* with a robust display of cultural richness, it was time for the church wedding. As a young girl, she had dreamt of a day like this when her Prince Charming will make her the cynosure of all eyes in a *talk-of-the-town* wedding.

st like in the many countless tribes in Nigeria and across Africa, the Igbos place a very high importance on their traditional wedding rites.

Certainly, she loved the idea that some were bound to be envious of her new status to a "rich" *di. Or who wouldn't want to get married to a well-to-do husband?* The usual scenery as you drove across town even appeared more beautiful on a *once-in-alifetime* day like this. The elaborate display of wealth quietly spoke of the trip she and her darling *suitor* took to Dubai in preparation for the joyous occasion.

Dubai is a choice destination for shopping trips abroad for those who can afford it. To go to Dubai to shop is a thing of class and prestige among the people.

Young beautiful ladies: A regular feature at a typical wedding ceremony.

With a bevy of beauties expressed in the damsels on display in the bridal train, and the exotic convoy of cars proudly displaying their brand names, the usual stress associated with driving through an urban centre like Aba didn't seem to matter today.

The love of cars becomes more evident when they are on display on such social events like this.

Patience is a virtue espoused in the holy scriptures. Priests in accordance with bibilical injunctions would often exemplify it more than others.

The retinue of priests were made to wait patiently and dutifuly at the cathedral as the long list of guests strolled in to join those already present. The atmosphere as the wedding ceremony went on can be described as picturesque. It was a wedding to remember.

CHAPTER TWO

Wedding, then the Marriage

AN AWAKENING SO REAL

Constant Arguements and fights are signs that something serious is desperately wrong.

No sooner had the marriage begun than the reality began to set in. It set in swifter than you would expect. The ageless demon called *irreconciliable differences* reared up its ugly head. To be honest however, in retrospect, it was always there even from when the fire of their *ifunaya* started. *Ahuru m gi na anya,* the expression of romantic feeling between the lovebirds was beginning to evaporate with the rapidity of a methylated spirit exposed to air. At this point, a Save-Our-Soul visit to a [marriage] counselor becomes the next thing, especially for the wife.

Reaching out for professional or spiritual help during crisis moment is always a step in the right direction.

"The marriage has become a living hell."

She sobs. Then she ranted endlessly about Eddie being irresponsible. He partied heavily. He was hardly home every other night. It was one mistress after another. Sometimes he even brought them home.

"Eddie carries his joblessness like a badge with pride." In addition, she was being verbally abused with his foul language on her—*Hateful and hurtful words too terrible for print.* His company had become a choking burden for her, and she just couldn't take it anymore. A classical tale of a sweet love gone sour. It was still like a bad dream and she wished she could just wake up from it. She wanted out. Period!

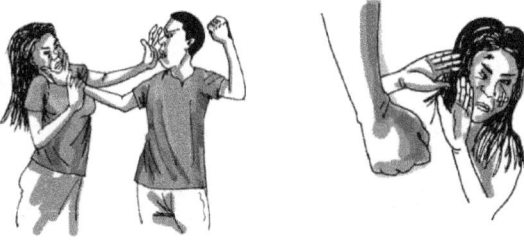

If you bother to check out the statistics today, you would be surprised at what is happening in many marriages.

After listening to her reasons for wanting out of the marriage, I informed her they were not sufficient enough to warrant such drastic a decision.

Telling the home truth is hardly an easy thing to do but it must be said with love, care and empathy

Her complain wasn't anything out of the ordinary. While they dated, Eddie *tantalized* and spoilt her with expensive gifts and trips abroad. It was a romance too good to be true and she was swept-off her feet often by the good times he gave her. Yet for all the goodies, she never bothered to ask him where the money he spent on her came from considering that she observed over time that Eddie mostly stayed indoors during the day and more importantly he didn't seem to have a particular line of work one could say he was involved in.

While we spoke, it was glaring that Eddie had always been a *die-hard* party animal. He drank a lot, smoked too and clubbing was one thing he enjoyed very much. He also had a reputation for being very flirtatious. He was an unrepentant womanizer who would chase after anything in skirt. Adaobi knew all these in a short time yet she made endless excuses for him convincing herself that she could, with her love, change him. Naively she expected that as time went by and Eddie got older and more mature, he would drop-off these unwholesome habits. Without realizing it, she had signed up for unending disappointments and constant heartbreaks. Eddie not only persisted in his ways, he got worse by and by. Needless to say, their marriage was now totally breaking apart with no solution in sight. She felt it was finally time she walked out of this *ordeal* called marriage!

I informed her that she shouldn't back out yet because marriage, according to the Word of God, is supposed to last a life time.

Changing a person is hardly an easy thing to do. Yet many women naively believe they can change their men.

Defiantly, she insisted she wanted to walk out. Justifying herself, she rebuffed my admonitions, telling me they were *easier said than done*. As far she was concerned, there was nothing keeping her in the marriage anymore.

"Adaobi, if you truly understand what marriage is in God's eyes and what it truly and really mean to be married according to God's word, you wouldn't even be

11

contemplating backing out now."

Those words seemed to stop her in her tracks as it caught her attention and aroused her curiousity. In response, she sobered up, "Pastor, please tell me something I don't know."

CHAPTER THREE

Why Should You Even Marry?

LOOKING THROUGH GOD'S MANUAL

The Pharisees in the days of Jesus would often seek to justify themselves because they thought they knew so much.

"One day the Pharisees were badgering him: "Is it legal for a man to divorce his wife for any reason?" He (Jesus) answered, "Haven't you read in your Bible that the Creator originally made man and woman for each other, male and female? And because of this, a man leaves father and mother and is firmly bonded to his wife, becoming one flesh—no longer two bodies but one. Because God created this organic union of the two sexes, no one should desecrate this art by cutting them apart. They shot back in rebuttal, "if that's so, why did Moses give instructions for divorce papers and divorce procedures?" Jesus said, Moses provided for divorce as concession to your hardheartedness, but it is not part of God's original plan"

— *Matthew 19:3-8 (The Message Bible).*

It is very clear from the conversation Jesus had with the pharisees that God's intention has always been that marriage would last for a life time. God's design for marriage is for it to last till the very end. This implies that Marriage must be much more serious than it may appear on the surface. The marriage institution should therefore only be entered into after a serious degree of careful consideration. Before you say those magical words "I DO", make sure you have sought wise counsel and carefully considered and deliberated on it. Any "mistake" afterwards could be considered a life-time regret with constant frustrations a reminder of your mistake — *unless God intervenes*.

When a person gets saved by accepting the lordship of Jesus Christ, it is no doubt the most important decision of a person's life. Sadly, so many still die everyday without making that decision. They found out only when it became too late, as they approach God's fierce judgement in eternity and it finally dawns on them that there is infact a scary place of torment too horrible to describe with words. Hell fire became real when it was too late to *repent and be saved*. (Acts 4:12)

However, for a person still alive and who has surrendered to Jesus Christ and has made him the lord and personal saviour, that decision remains the most important decision to be made.

In death, there's no turning back. It is final. Judgement awaits. We should have similar mindset with marriage. There's no going back.

Next to that decision would be the *choice* of Marriage. Beloved, it is that serious and never to be taken casually. Marriage is a very serious institution that has farreaching implications spiritually, psychologically, culturally and socially. It is not a concept to be handled with levity.

Marriage is no joke. It's serious business. The demands are real and could be tough every now and then. Sometimes, it's not fun at all. Therefore, discrete caution and care must be employed when deciding who to marry.

Marriage signifies the fusing together of two individuals to become one indivisible unit. If you jump in carelessly, you will most likely jump out with serious psychological, emotional bruises and injuries.

In commercial transactions, businesses and organizations would often do *duedilgence* on the person or institution they want to transact with. In similar fashion, the business of getting married and staying successfully married would even require more serious due-diligence. While a business relationship can come to an abrupt end and the parties involved severe ties, counting their loss and gains, the ties in a marriage relationship are much more complicated and complex to just break like that.

Good businesses do due-diligence. Good marriage-to-be should do even more.

Marriage isn't another business transaction. It is a profound and mysterious spiritual reality beyond the anatomy of two people who share the same bed. Any attempt to break it automatically results in pains and trauma that are better imagined than experienced. Even a prolonged strain in a *"normal"* marriage where both are still willing and mutually-committed, if let unaddressed, creates enough pain. How much more when one party wants out because of *irreconcilable differences* arising from the *foundational* issues as seen in the case of Adaobi and Eddie's. The foundational issues sometimes are enough to point out clearly that a marriage should never have taken place in the first place.

If you are going to spend the rest of your life with

someone in a marriage, you should take your time and do all the duediligence you possibly can. There's never need to hurry about it. I dare say that even beyond the choice of your career, the choice of marriage holds more significance. You can always change a career. People switch careers at some point for various reasons. In a marriage, things are much more intricate.

You can always change a career. You can even change a lover. It's not so easy to "change" a marriage for another one.

Beyond the facade of being married, it may surprise you to know the statistics regarding people who are or might be enduring their marriage or who are just staying put there for cultural reasons or societal expectations. God designed marriage to be a blessing. A *blessing* is not something you endure or just get by with. It is something to be enjoyed and cherished and to serve a divine purpose to the glory of God himself.

Don't be another statistic of those just enduring being married. You have a responsibility to yourself and to the God who created and called you to Himself to be happy and fulfilled in this life. You must know right so you can choose right. When the purpose of a thing is not known, then abuse is inevitable. God says "my people are *destroyed* for lack of knowledge. (Hosea 4:6)." Your decision is governed by the quality of information that is available to you. It is purpose that determines what you look out for in a partner. Purpose determines choice.

First of all, we must always remember this simple yet *profound* truth that marriage was and still is God's idea. God invented it. Man only tries to understand and master it. However to really understand it the way it should be understood, only God can explain best because he invented it. The divine purpose of marriage can therefore not be discovered nor understood correctly from the pages of celebrity magazines or online gossip blogs. Hollywood, Bollywood or Nollywood can not provide much either. These are sources of cultural entertainment but they hardly reflect or give God's view on the subject of marriage.

As the inventor of Marriage, God obviously has a perfect mastery of it. If you want to know the purpose of a product, the best person to ask would and should be the maker or manufacturer of that product. Often, the information would be put in a *manual*. Since God invented marriage, he must be the best person to ask on what it is and how it works well optimally according to design. Whatever God has to say on marriage is found in the manual he *inspired* men to write on his behalf. This manual which we call the *Holy Bible* contains God's thoughts, ideas and blue print on just about everything that concerns life and how we are to live it — *and that includes marriage too!* His will for marriage and how it should be conducted and maintained is found in his word in the Holy Scriptures. His *word* is his *will* revealed to us. To discover his will, we must diligently search his word daily.

CHAPTER FOUR

Settle with Yourself First

YOUR PERSONAL REASONS MATTER TOO!

As the crown of God's creation, the human is created to reason. God made man to be like him in image and likeness. Being conscious of that will help you not to be passive or foolish in making decisions.

As a rational being, you were created to reason. What makes the human uniquely different from all other creatures of God is the fact that God made man in his image and likeness, hence man had to be given a soul. As a living soul, man possesses the capacity to reason and act by himself in self-will. That was why when the first man fell, it was an exercise of self-will in his soul against the will of God. The soul is the centre in a person where logic, reason, emotions and will are situated.

When you're born-again, your soul which was formerly

lost to sinfulness is being renewed in the light of God's word. The soul begins to get aligned to God's way of seeing and doing things. Therefore, in making a marriage decision, understand that your soul *faculty* is an active participant in your decision-making process. Let your soul be *full* and *robust* with godly knowledge, wisdom and instruction. Let this godliness guide your reasoning and your ability to ask the real questions that matter. When real questions are asked and they are clear and well-framed in your thinking, the right answers will be sought out.

The truth is that as a woman, you can not really submit the way you should, except you're following and helping to build a dream together i.e. his mission! Submission is broken into two parts — "sub" and "mission" . To "sub" is **to come under** whereas "mission" is **to be up to something** *i.e.* to have a vision or to be fixed on a purpose or an assignment.

Therefore, where there is no real purpose expressed in having a vision or mission, there really isn't anything to submit to.

When you're up to something that your life is centered around, you are bound to be strategic about it as you proceed on the journey.

Ask yourself the real questions that matter. They will provoke the real answers to come out addressing the foundational issues .

Life is full of obstacles and unexpected events, so you adapt to changes as they come. This you do with the intelligent use of your mind. Assessing available data in the face of changing events or circumstance and constantly being able to always arrive at a reasonable conclusion on what next to do is a *skill* any focused and reasonable human being should be able develop and master throughout one's lifetime.

CHAPTER FIVE

The Basic Thing to Begin with

FRUITFUL. MULTIPLY. INCREASE

This first diligence check is very basic and it begins here.

#Diligence Check:

What are the chances of increasing and multiplying together?

Perhaps, your mind is going to whether the man is able to get a woman pregnant or whether the woman is able to get pregnant. That is obviously important because procreation is an important purpose of marriage. Marriage is the only legitimate avenue of procreation for believers. The bible outrightly abhors same-sex marriage (*Lev. 18:22, 20:13, Rom.1:26-27*). Moreover a same-sex marriage can never lead to fulfilment in procreation.

Beyond biological proceation, to increase in number means to proliferate, to multiply and to reproduce your kind.

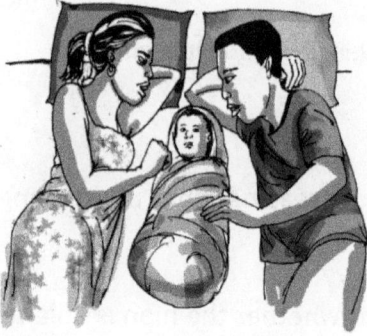

Bringing a child into this world is symbolic of the power of a man and a woman working together in harmony to achieve great things.

The woman is a *suitable* help for the man. As a woman, you are to be a help to an already *existing* ability. When choosing your life partner, you must find out if the person has a *sense* of his God-given *domain* in life. That will determine his ability to manifest fruitfulness, multiply, and increase. His God-given domain also raises the question of whether you're suitable as partners or not.

How do you ascertain whether your potential suitor has a sense of his God-given domain? Look out for his *willingness* to take *responsibility* for his life. When you're in your domain, all your innate qualities to make it better comes alive. You become a leader first of yourself and a good steward of resources —material or human—placed in your care.

Because he's leading himself, he will be a better leader for you. There can be no multiplication unless there is good leadership. Leadership is an art that anybody can learn but goals are not learnt. They are conceived based on a sense of purpose and vision. Goals when conceived are set in achieveable terms. To achieve those goals, relationships are consciously built, people are deliberately brought into the picture. While all these are happening, character and integrity are being tested. A leading man takes responsibility in creating the atmosphere that inspire and motivate people around him to respond to working together in order to achieve greater good that will benefit and bless all. But it all starts with having clearly-defined goals in life. So ask yourself, *does he have set goals in life?* What is he really up to doing with his life? What is he really trying to achieve with his time, energy and resources? Are they consistent with his sense of his God-given domain?

A written-down goal shows seriousness, focus and purpose.

If you marry someone who has no sense of his God-given domain, hence no vision and nothing he's really up to and no clearly-defined goals, hence no need to develop and unleash his leadership potential, when the constant changes of life come like they do, they leave him further confused, sinking him more into emptiness and misery. You as a woman get stuck and frustrated with him. He is not offering any real leadership because he doesn't know what he should be up to. It can really wear you out when you're trying to find a new direction for yourself and your supposedleader is not even cooperating. Instead, it is arguement and fight every time. Life will be miserable for you because both of you can't agree on real issues unless you become like that person — *satisfied with going nowhere.*

Fixing a bearing and setting your sail before the storm of unexpected changes in life means he can stay strong in the face of uncertainty because there's always a focus.

Adaobi, like every woman, was looking to her husband for inspiration, motivation and direction. This she could only get if her life and work was contributing to what Eddie was up to. Eddie really wasn't up to anything. He had no sense of his God-given domain. He had missed the first foundational issue. He had no relationship with God and he wasn't serious about establishing one. Adaobi, on the other hand overlooked that. The gifts and the good times seemed to matter to her more as their relationship progressed. That was her first *mistake*. Every other foundational issue builds on this one.

CHAPTER SIX

The Business of Communicating

HE CAN'T OR HE WON'T?

#Diligence Check:
How is the Communication like?

Communication is the live-wire of any relationship. It is not a cut-and-paste matter, it carries different shades to it. Communication combines layers of verbal and nonverbal elements.

A man who is up to something worthwhile in life will realize in time that it takes building strong relationships to get there. Character and integrity will be tested in a relationship over and over. As a good and strong leader that he is suppose to be, his communication is something you must always watch out for.

Effective communication is the live-wire of any healthy relationship. Each person is an individual with uniqueness. Therefore, communication style vary from person to person. However, regardless of what his communication style is, if the relationship is worth it, then he must always find a way to express his thoughts and positions on issues that concern you — *and both of you together!*

Communication requires diligence, patience and understanding from both parties. Some people are fond of not saying what is on their mind, thereby frustrating the other party. They often would expect the other person to figure it out as if that person was a mind reader.

Many of the problems in relationships and marriage stem from the lack of effective communication. How are you supposed to be an effective partner when you don't even know where both of you are going together? How would you contribute and how would you know what is expected of you per time? Not being able to communicate effectively is in itself a problem. If he doesn't see it as a problem to be addressed and worked on, then it becomes a real foundation issue that will never go away and will always put a strain on the relationship, jeopardizing your long-term happiness together.

Lack of communication is like two people facing opposite direction without realizing it.

Lack of effective communication usually woud lead to unhealthy communication patterns like psychological bullying and even violent conduct in a relationship.

Frustrated people have a tendency to be violent. One can be frustrated from time to time when you're reaching for a goal and it's not working out at the moment. To however be without a sense of mission neglecting your God-given purpose in life means there's hardly any fulfilment to look forward to. To fill the void and emptiness, a person will turn to other things. Clearly Eddie was void and empty. The changes in fortune further showed the futility of the things he had hoped on. He couldn't communicate his frustrations to his wife. Cowardly, violence became his way out. Sadly too, Adaobi had no idea what she was up against.

CHAPTER SEVEN

Respect is Always Golden

SELFLESS OR SELF-SERVING?

#Diligence Check:
How is his respect like?

Respect is self-generated. If you exude self-respect, you will manifest it in your relationship.

Y ou can not give what you don't have. A self-respecting   person will also give some respect to others around him. How well you respect yourself is predicated on your *self-esteem* which is based on your *self-worth* which stems out of your *awareness* of what your life is really about according to God's purpose for your life. Eddie had none or too little of it. That was why he threw his life about in worth-less debauchery, hence he couldn't really cherish his most prized asset, his wife. As a woman, watch how the man treats others especially those of lesser status than him. It often indicates how respectful he is and how he will eventually treat you because you're going to be under his authority. It is easy to treat a person right when you want something from then, but what happens afterwards? What if you didn't want or need anything of worth from them, will you still accord them maximum respect?

A person can pretend to be respectful but disrespect doesn't take long to show itself. How he treats people of lesser status says a lot about his character and how he would likely treat you later on

Much of our success depends on how well we get along with others. Therefore, the ability to accommodate the differing view of others say a lot about the person's character. A leader worth following or working with should possess a well-demonstrated history of respect for views differing from his. The person must have the ability to respect other people's ideas, preferences, feelings and wellbeing. This person must not be selfish. Selfish people are so full of themselves which makes them very manipulative. You must find out whether the person is a self-loathing "Chief" or an amiable "Servant-leader". When he is a "Chief", he is self-serving and believes that everybody must make sacrifices for him; making personal sacrifices is a secondary issue while he feels entitled to others shifting grounds for him. This kind of person can be described as megalomaniac. A servant leader on the other hand lives to serve, always looking for ways to create comfort around his partner.

He disrespected them   It's only a matter of time

History is powerful and has a way of repeating itself if lessons are not learnt from it. If He has constantly shown disrespect to people or has a reputation for not treating others well, his love, charm and charisma is only a facade which will fade away with time. You are in for a rough time and your regret will not be minimal at all.

The height of disrespect for your wife is to bring another woman into your house and on your matrimonial bed. No reason whatsoever, justifies that. Eddie's action shows that all the while they dated and gallivanted around having the *good* times, he inherently never really had any iota of respect for Adaobi. Unfortunately, when a woman is too carried away with the good times and the illusions that come with it, she fails to see what she ought to be seeing. The signs were always there and carelessly she *failed* to pick up that signal.

CHAPTER EIGHT

An Enjoyable Companion?

SPIRIT. SOUL. BODY

#Diligence Check:
Does he have good front-end personality? How much of a good companion is he?

The first marriage was in the garden of Eden. God brought both of them together to offer companionship to each other.

A ccording to Genesis 2:18, God says that it was not good for the man to be alone. God designed marriage

to satisfy the man's need for companionship. He made a helpmeet suitable to him. This need cannot be effectively met unless we understand the nature of man. Man is a spirit that has a soul and lives in a body. It therefore follows that in choosing a life partner, the person must be able to provide companionship on these three levels— spirit, soul and body.

Your **Spirit** refers to that part of you that enables you to have a relationship with and communicate with God. When you accept Jesus Christ as your personal Lord and saviour, your spirit is awakened by the eternal life of God that enters into it. It becomes regenerated! Since companionship in a personal relationship is required on three levels of spirit, soul and body, your partner must equally be a person who has experienced that regeneration in his spirit. Otherwise, there can be no effective spiritual companionship. Marriage is first spiritual before anything else, therefore it must be spiritually discerned by *spiritually-awakened* partners.

One major reason Marriages are in trouble today is because there is a spiritual *disconnect* between the partners. The Bible philosophically asks if any relationship can exist between light and darkness or if life and death can have a relationship. Any person that has not made a conscious decision to accept Jesus as His Lord and Saviour is spiritually-dead and you have no business having a personal relationship with that person. If you marry such a person, it will be like lying down in the same bed with a dead person (romancing the dead). It is called **spiritual necrophilia.**

God is love and he designed marriage to model his love for man. Therefore love must be a spiritual thing; A *spiritually-regenerated* person has received God's love *shed abroad in his heart* (Romans 5:5), therefore he can truly love. On the other hand, a spiritually-unregenerated person has a spiritually-dead spirit.

It is absolutely necessary that both the man and the woman in a personal relationship are spiritually regenerated. In otherwords, they must be born-again christians.

Wearing expensive make-up or designer clothings can not

fulfil the need for spiritual companionship. Be certain your partner is someone who has experienced the new spiritual birth in Christ Jesus. In additon, he should be someone with whom you share the same spiritual devotion and beliefs.

I once had the opportunity to meet a lady who complained that her husband insisted that she stopped any form of fervent praying in his house. She said her husband would become very uneasy whenever she started to pray. It was obvious that they did not have any form of *spiritual compatibility*, hence spiritual companionship was virtually non-existent. This man would maltreat, abuse and deprive this woman of basic needs. She *suffered* so much that she had to run away to save herself from his cruelty.

Where there is spiritual companionship, you would regularly pray and worship God together, study God's word together, attend church and participating in one form or the other of spiritual service will become something you enjoy together.

With the **soul**, comes intellectual yearning and cognitive abilities. To have true and effective companionship at the soul level, your partner must be one who excites you intellectually. You want to be intellectually entertained when you commune and have fellowship together. When there is no enjoyment in soul companionship, the tendency is to begin to be *emotionally promiscous.* This is perhaps one reason we often see men who are married to beautiful women having dalliances with other women who are not even as beautiful as their wife.

Marriage requires both minds working together in having conversations in discussion, planning, strategizing, networking and socializing, choice of entertainment etc. A potential spouse must possess a level of intellectual and cognitive expression that enables for enjoyable and effective companionship. If this is missing, you are always prone to feeling lonely or isolated in that relationship. Imagine living with a person who reasons and thus behaves immaturely. You will end up treating that person accordingly. This could explain why some married people complain of how their partners disrespect them or keep things from them. There's that tendency to start feeling inadequate, not good enough or not being on the same *level* as the other person. It can hurt a lot leaving the *affected* person constantly angry. Like any typical foundational issue, it never goes away just like that. It will continue to persist until both parties are willing to sit down and address it. It requires great patience and even at that, it is a complex matter that is not easily solved. Better to avoid it while you still can, if you're yet to marry.

I remember this couple that I used to know. The man had very little formal education while the wife was very educated. As you would expect, they just couldn't jell intellectually. Their cognitive abilities and reasoning were a world-apart. They couldn't maintain the same social network. The man always felt insecure and because of this feeling of inferiority, he began to bring unfounded and unreasonable accusations against his wife. The man would complain incessantly that his wife didn't respect him. He would accuse his wife of using "big grammar" to mess him.

You know as water must find its level, the man started looking for companionship with ladies on his level, a typical case of *emotional adultery*—a situation where a partner begins to confide in someone of the opposite sex other than their partner. Needless to say, the marriage caused a lot of pain and discomfort to both parties and their families. It later broke down irretrievably.

For a man, being married to a far-more intellectually-superior woman can make him feel like a dwarf in the relationship. The tendency to always "look out" is even greater, thus jeopardizing the marriage.

Sharing good companionship at the level of the spirit is good, however, companionship also extends into the soul level. You must be able to communicate and connect on that plane too.

The Attitude matters. Infact, it's almost everything. An intelligent person with a positive attltude is simply irresistible and will likely make a good companion. Arrogant, selfish and saucy people should be avoided. The person must be someone who makes you feel good about yourself. It must be someone who excites, challenges and complements you. Avoid *supercilious* persons who make you feel inferior or unimportant. They will always elicit negative emotions from you. There is no better time than now to *recalibrate* and take more seriously your intellectual and personal development. Regardless of where you are at the moment or what you have been through, develop yourself and keep at it. It's better late than never.

While you contemplate on your future with somebody, do not neglect your personal development. Seize the moment maximizing every opportunity to become a better and more balanced person. Consciously seek to develop your *emotional* intelligence so that you can assess life, people and events better as they unfold in your life.

We are admonished in the holy bible to *not be conformed to this world but to be transformed by the renewal of the mind (Romans 12:1-2).*

Beloved, the mind is a terrible thing to waste. Invest in yourself to become a better asset to people in your life.

Build your soul by making it robust with the right content. Feed it with the word of God and intellectually-stimulating knowledge from decent materials in the form of books, research journals, healthy media content online and offline. Use the internet smartly and wisely. You have enormous amount of information right at your fingertips at the mere click of a button.

Do you like the package before you?

Your partner, in **bodily** form or shape, should be someone that makes your heart skip a beat; someone who you are physically attracted to. When Adam saw Eve, his heart skipped some beats and all he could say was "This is the bone of my bones and the flesh of my flesh, this is who I have been searching for." If you perceive someone as unprepossessing, don't venture into a marriage relationship with that person.

There must be something about that person that excites your loins. As a lady, you ought to prepare yourself for what you desire in a man. Keep yourself bodily attractive just as you look for what you're sensually attracted by in a man.

The human body is controlled by the five senses — *sight, touch, smell, taste, hearing*

Sight: Do you like what you see? Women are moved by what they hear the same way men are moved by what they see. So here, more of the discussion is on the lady. A wise saying goes this way: *Who you are is so loud I can't hear what you're saying.*

In otherwords, perception is so powerful it controls how your words are received and processed by the receiver.

In a romantic relationship, we show care and committment all the time, we learn to trust step-by-step, we make reasonable demands when necessary, we reach compromises at other times, we expect understanding regularly, we plead for adjustment when needed, we demonstrate patience constantly, etc.

Don't set yourself up for failure or a dismal performance by a poor sense of dressing and presentation. Package yourself well. Eat well to be healthy and dress proper to be respected. Modesty is always a better and safer route to travel in. Shun nudity and lewdness. *Don't dress like a suspect and expect to be treated like a prospect.* Essential beauty tips like manicures, pedicures, facials and the use of body moisturizers are good things to use.

Touch: How do you want to be touched? You have a right to demand that your man be a gentleman in his mannerism especially towards you. A rough, coarse, impatient and uncaring way of touching you shows a lack of respect for you and gentlemanliness. It can be a sign that bodily companionship in the relationship going forward will always be an issue.

Smell: You can judge a man by his smell. Beloved, how a man smells can tell you a lot about him; how he smells is indicative of whether he cares about himself or not.

If he does not care about himself, it will be almost impossible for him to care about your grooming. I am not sure any reasonable person would want to hug a smelly fish.

Taste: Your taste vs. His Appreciation Have a good taste and let it radiate in your personality. Then watch for his appreciation of your taste. How sensitive or insensitive is he to your taste. A good taste leaves a good feeling in the mouth. If a man can not recognize and appreciate this over time, then he has some issues to fix in his life. An insensitive man can not offer good companionship. Being constantly insensitive is like having a foul smelling mouth. It's a sign of being emotionally lazy. This means you don't bother to find out the effect of your actions on those closest to you. How would you like to kiss a foul-smelling mouth all the days of your life? Not a pleasant prospect.

Hearing: Words make or break. Out of the abundance of the heart, the mouth speaks. The heart of a man is revealed in the kind of words that comes out of his mouth. Watch out for qualities of being refined in his speech. Behaviours of being indiscrete, vulgar or profane is not a good sign of a good companion.

Packaging creates expectation and excitement. Through constant packaging, you can maintain positive expectation and the right excitement in your relationship.

Bad communication corrupts good manners. Relationship is not a place of bondage but a place to release your potential to be a better person and do things better.

From the spirit to the soul and to the body, you must find this person enjoyable and fun to converse and be with. There must be sparks in the way both of you handle each other. There must be a flow that transcends through the three levels of spirit, soul and body.

CHAPTER NINE

While You're Still Waiting

VALUE YOURSELF BETTER

#Diligence Check:

Is he really interested in you—Spirit, Soul and Body? Or is it just for the sex?

Unfortunately, most people today seek companionship only for the sex. Dearest, sex alone can not keep a marriage. When the only reason he is getting married to you is because of the size of your breasts or how curvaceous your hips are, what happens if he sees someone who is "sexier" in the future? What happens when the things that used to be robust and firm are no longer the way it used to be because of age or the results of childbearing?

A lady complained to me that her husband has not touched her sexually since she had their first baby. She said it seems as if her husband can no longer stand her. I found out that bodily companionship was all that they shared together. When childbearing took its toll on the body of the woman, the only thing that attracted the husband to her disappeared and he started to seek bodily companionship with a "fresher" body.

How do you know whether your body is all that he is interested in?

If how *sexy* you are is all he talks about when you are with him? If your *body* is the only part of you that he is *interested* in meeting or interacting with? If *sexy underwears* are the only *gifts* he likes to give you? If the bedroom is his *best* place in the apartment any time you are around? These and many more may be *signs* that he is only interested in you because of bodily companionship.

Child-bearing can take its toll on a woman's body. If he was only interested in the sex, it begins to show as he looks out for newer gratification

While you wait, don't be in a hurry. Don't rush your decision. Instead, value yourself more and get to know yourself better. Celebrate yourself. Learn how to feel good about yourself at all times. Maintain that posture. If you perceive yourself as attractive, others will mostly likely perceive you in the same light.

CHAPTER TEN

Wedding not Same as Marriage

EVENT VS. EXPERIENCE

As we rounded-off our discussion in my office, Adaobi heaved a *heavy* sigh of regret. "Pastor, now I know that I am the Architect of my misfortune." She admits. "I wish I knew this earlier. I wish I had known how to do my due diligence check before I said "I do" ." came the sad note. "I was caught up in the euphoria of the moment. I just wanted to get married without understanding what it really meant." She expressing her regret. "I was more interested in the trips abroad, in the gifts and the frequent outings."

Embarrassed at her own admission. "I was captivated by his looks and never bothered to find out and study the content of his character" came the tired voice. "My attention was more on just getting married and not on the marriage after the wedding. I was never prepared. I jumped blindly into the marriage and now, I am left to regret my actions."

"Pastor, can you help me? What do I do now? Where do I go from here?" She sobs

In committing yourself to marriage, it is better to wait than to be sorry afterwards.

Beloved, in these trying times, you can save yourself a whole lot of unnecessary pain, frustration and heartache. The problem of finding yourself in a "wrong" marriage is not so easy to solve. Marriage is a very serious concept that should not be dabbled into carelessly.

It is always better and wiser to learn from the experiences of others than to experience the regret yourself.

One has to exercise a high degree of care and inquisitiveness. I know that one can not completely predict human behavior, but that does not absolve one from the responsibility of making some reasonable inquiries before committing to a lifetime partnership. The bible declares that *"He who finds a wife finds a good thing* and obtains favour of the LORD"—(*Proverbs18:22*); This presupposes that some searching and choosing is required.

Dearest, preparing for a good wedding obviously requires a lot. However, after the wedding ceremony is over, the marriage begins. One is an event, the other is an experience you live in and come to terms with. It is the *aggregate* character of the people in that marriage that will ensure whether or not a good marriage will be built.

If you break a good egg and mix with a bad or spoilt egg, you will still end up with a *bad omlette*. If you think of yourself as having a good character, please ensure that your partner-to-be is also of a good or even better character. A good and godly character is an important trait to look out for in a potential life partner.

Trying to fry a good and a spoilt egg together offers a good lesson in character.

Material gifts will eventually get old or may even be stolen. Memories of the good times you had together on your numerous trips will be become distant at some point. Character however, is an ever-present reality you will be dealing with all the days of your life together.

The Bible teaches that those *who are led by the spirit of God are the sons of God* (**Romans 8:14**). I pray that the eyes of your understanding be opened and enlightened by the Spirit of the living God (*Ephesians 1:15-21*), so that you will not make that mistake. *You will choose your right partner. You will not be deceived or misled in Jesus' name!* **Marriage** is a very important decision you will make in your life and the consequences of a bad or faulty marriage affects almost every sphere of your life. Take your time. Learn from others. Don't be blinded by the emotions of wrecklessly *falling in love*. Love is not enough. There are make-orbreak *issues* that goes with it. Check things out properly. Do your due diligence. Don't be a *victim* of rushing things.

(+) *Quiz*

From this small book, what are the four basic things you should look out for in a potential marriage partner? If you had to add three more things, what would they be?

....
....
....
....
....
....
....
....
....
....
....
....
....
....
....
....
....
....
....
....
....
....
....
....

(-) *Quiz*

From this small book, can you deduce seven to ten behaviours you should not tolerate in a potential marriage partner?

....
....
....
....
....
....
....
....
....
....
....
....
....
....
....
....
....
....
....
....
....
....
....
....

*This is the first in the **"Don't Marry Him Yet"** series.*

*Join the **DON'T MARRY HIM YET** conversation online on the social media platforms:*
Instagram. Twitter. Snapchat. Youtube. Google+

#DontMarrryHimYet
@DontMarryHimYet

You can reach Anny Ikebudu via email:
pastoranny@yahoo.com

*You can have personal audience with him by following **Anny Ikebudu** on Twitter and Facebook.*

Telephone: +2348033207242